The Primary Comprehension Toolkit

Strategy Book 4: Infer and Visualize

Lessons

In the Toolkit, we emphasize reading to explore and learn about the world.

In this Strategy Book, the lessons for inferring and visualizing are:

Lesson 12 . . . . **page 2**
Infer Meaning:
  *Merge background knowledge
  with clues from the text*

Lesson 13 . . . . **page 18**
Learn to Visualize:
  Get a picture in your mind

Lesson 14 . . . . **page 32**
Make Sense of New Information:
  *Infer from features, pictures,
  and words*

Lesson 15 . . . . **page 46**
**Infer and Visualize with
Narrative Nonfiction:**
  Tie thinking to the text

Strategy Support

Strategy Wrap-up **64**

Assessment Checklist **65**

Annotated Rubric **66**

Thinksheets **67**

Inferring is the bedrock of understanding. Writers don't always spill information onto the page; often they leak it slowly, leaving clues along the way to keep the reader engaged in the act of constructing meaning. Inferring involves taking what you know, your background knowledge, and merging it with clues in the text to come up with some information that isn't explicitly stated there. Inferential thinking helps readers figure out unfamiliar words, draw conclusions, make interpretations, make predictions, surface big ideas, and even create mental images.

Visualizing is sort of a first cousin to inferring. When readers visualize, they construct meaning by creating mental images— seeing, hearing, tasting, touching, and even smelling! Younger children seem particularly inclined to visualize in support of understanding as they listen to and read stories, often living through or living in the stories. When young children infer and visualize as they listen, read, and view, they respond with joy, surprise, or even dread. Inferring and visualizing allow learners to expand their thinking and get at the deeper meaning in text.

D0503413

DEDICATED TO TEACHERS™

Library of Congress Cataloging-in-Publication Data
CIP data on file with the Library of Congress

Infer and Visualize
ISBN-13: 978-0-325-02151-5
ISBN-10: 0-325-02151-1

Primary Comprehension Toolkit: Language and Lessons for Active Literacy
ISBN-13: 978-0-325-00997-1
ISBN-10: 0-325-00997-X

Printed in the United States of America on acid-free paper

14 13   ML   5

Lesson 12

Infer Meaning

Text Matters

Here is another example of how we use all genres to teach comprehension to little ones. When teaching younger kids to infer, poetry is a great place to begin. Poetry is short—compared to a novel anyway! Poetry, by its very nature, leaves a lot to the imagination. The poet leaves clues in the poem, and readers merge those clues with their background knowledge to make meaning. When launching inferring, we choose poetry that kids can relate to, so that they can use their background knowledge to help them understand. We look for short poems, with several sections, or stanzas, each of which offers a puzzle to interpret—to infer through. Finally we most often choose poems that are fun and rhythmic, so kids really enjoy them.

Resources & Materials

Lesson Text

"Things" from *Honey, I Love and other love poems* by Eloise Greenfield (HarperCollins Publishers, 1978) [Available in the Trade Book Pack.]

Classroom Supplies
- "Things" Anchor Chart
- Chart paper and marker

Student Supplies
- Clipboard and pencil
- *I Infer* Thinksheets with different amounts of writing space [See *Strategy Book 4*, pages 67–69, or the DVD-ROM.]

Merge background knowledge with clues from the text

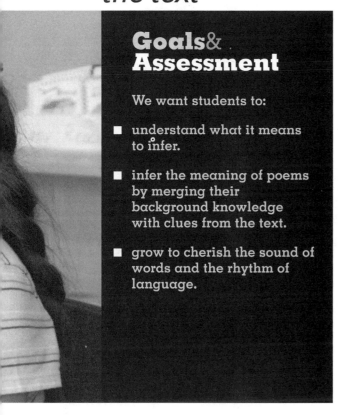

Goals& Assessment

We want students to:

- understand what it means to infer.

- infer the meaning of poems by merging their background knowledge with clues from the text.

- grow to cherish the sound of words and the rhythm of language.

Why&What

Inferring is at the heart of reading and thinking. Writers don't always spill information onto the page; often they leak it slowly, leaving clues along the way to keep the reader engaged in the act of constructing meaning. Inferring involves merging what you know, your background knowledge, with clues in the text to come up with information that isn't explicitly stated. Poetry is a great genre to launch a lesson about inferring. When we read or hear poetry, we understand more completely by thinking inferentially.

How

Connect and Engage

- Share the cover of the book and flip through the poems, explaining that the book is a collection of poems by one author.
- Have kids turn and talk about what they know about poetry.
- Read the poem aloud rhythmically.
- Read the poem together, with kids echoing the lines as you say them.

Model

- Explain that readers often have to infer the meaning of poetry to understand it.
- Share that *inferring* is taking background knowledge and adding clues from the text to it in order to figure something out.
- Place Post-its of inferences on a chart of the poem.

Guide

- Read another section of the poem and invite kids to draw or write what they infer is going on.
- Invite kids to share their inferences, first with a partner and then the whole group.

Practice Independently

- Read the last section and infer the meaning of it.
- Invite kids to jot down or draw what they infer on thinksheets.

Share the Learning

- Invite kids to share their inferences, either orally or with their thinksheets.
- Read the poem one last time.

Lesson Text

Eloise Greenfield's *Honey, I Love and other love poems* is an extraordinary collection that kids can't get enough of. The verses get kids up and moving as they gleefully read them in unison. They are ideal for teaching inferring. We selected the poem "Things" from the collection to model inferring. To understand this poem, kids need to think inferentially in each stanza of the poem, as well as in the overall poem, to get at the underlying ideas. Most importantly, kids' attention doesn't flag when we choral read this and the other wonderful poems because of their great rhythms, rhymes, and spirited language.

From *Honey, I Love and other love poems*, by Eloise Greenfield. Text copyright © 1978 by Eloise Greenfield. Used by permission of HarperCollins Publishers.

TEACHING MOVES	TEACHING LANGUAGE

Connect and Engage

Share the cover of the book and flip through the poems, explaining that the book is a collection of poems by one author.

I brought this wonderful book of poems. It is tiny, but great poems often come in small packages! *Honey, I Love and other love poems* is written by the poet Eloise Greenfield. All of the poems were written by her. This book is a collection of her poetry.

Have kids turn and talk about what they know about poetry.

Turn to each other and talk about what you know about poetry. *[Kids turn and talk.]* Tell me, what are some things you already know about poetry?

Hannah: It rhymes.

Some of it does, good noticing.

Sophie: It makes me laugh.

Some of it definitely makes us laugh. There are a lot of funny poems. I guess it could also make us sad. It depends on the poem, doesn't it?

Jamil: It is different than stories.

Say more about that, Jamil.

Jamil: You have to look with a poet's eye and hear with a poet's ear.

Wow! So beautiful what you are saying. What makes you think that?

Jamil: Our teacher showed us. Poetry sounds different than stories, the words sound different when we say them.

I agree with you, Jamil. Poetry does sound different than stories. One of the things I love about poetry is that it has rhythm.

Read the poem aloud rhythmically.

I selected this poem called "Things" from the collection and wrote it on a chart so you can all see it. Let me read it once for you. Listen to the rhythm. *[I read from the chart rhythmically. I read the last stanza more quietly and slowly.]*

Let's try it together. Let's say it as though you are the echo. I will say the line first and then you say a line. *[Kids echo each line after I read it.]*

Steph: Went to the corner

Kids: Went to the corner

Steph: Walked in the store

Kids: Walked in the store

Steph: Bought me some candy

Kids: Bought me some candy

Steph: Ain't got it no more

Kids: Ain't got it no more

Steph: Went to the beach

Kids: Went to the beach

Steph: Played on the shore

Kids: Played on the shore

Steph: Built me a sandhouse

Kids: Built me a sandhouse

Steph: Ain't got it no more

Kids: Ain't got it no more

Steph: Went to the kitchen

Kids: Went to the kitchen

Steph: Lay down on the floor

Kids: Lay down on the floor

Steph: Made me a poem

Kids: Made me a poem

Steph: Still got it

Kids: Still got it

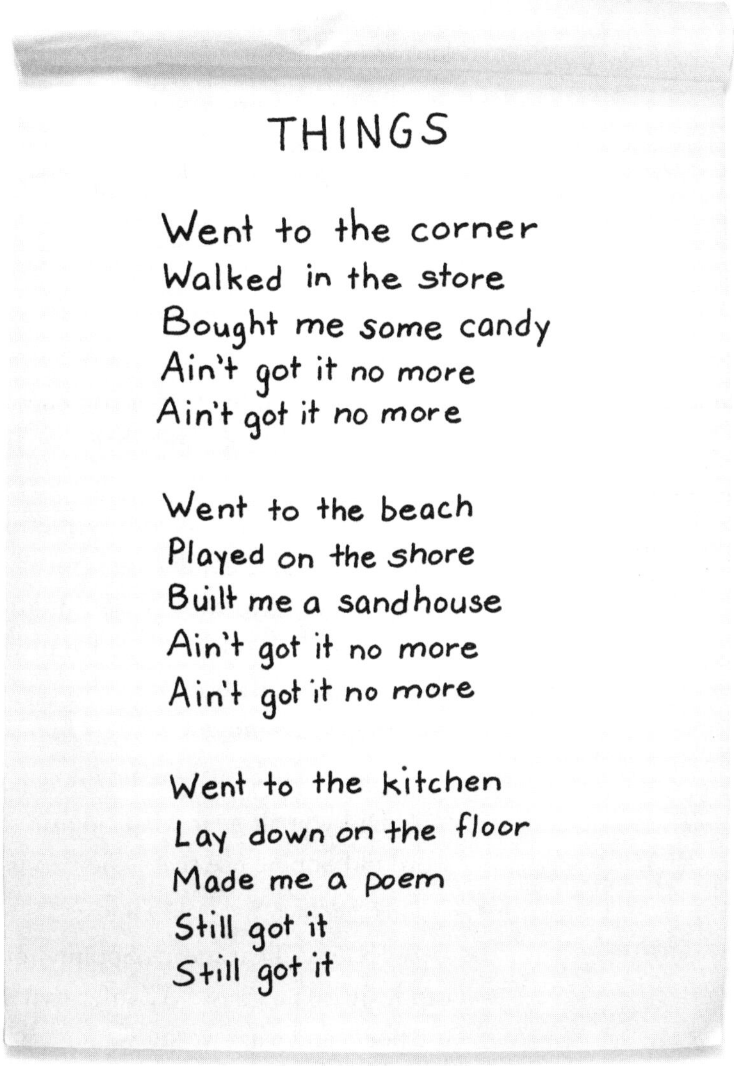

THINGS

Went to the corner
Walked in the store
Bought me some candy
Ain't got it no more
Ain't got it no more

Went to the beach
Played on the shore
Built me a sandhouse
Ain't got it no more
Ain't got it no more

Went to the kitchen
Lay down on the floor
Made me a poem
Still got it
Still got it

That was great. Want to try it again? *[All of them enthusiastically agree. We recite the poem again. Some are now saying the lines when I am. Others are echoing the lines, whichever is more comfortable for them.]* I just love that poem. How about you? *[Kids nod.]*

Model

Explain that readers often have to infer the meaning of poetry to understand it.

Let's think about this poem for a minute, and then we will read it again. Sometimes poetry doesn't give you all of the information; you have to figure it out. We call that *inferring*. For instance, I have a question. What happened to the candy? *[Hands wave in the air.]* Hang on a minute. You may know the answer, but the poem doesn't tell us. You have to infer. Who thinks they know? Sophie?

Sophie: She ate the candy.

So interesting. Let's take a look at that part. *[I point to the first stanza and read it. Kids join in spontaneously.]* Right here, where it says *Bought me some candy/Ain't got it no more*, it doesn't say what she did with the candy. It only says she doesn't have it anymore. What makes you think she ate it?

Sophie: That's what you do with candy!

Exactly, Sophie!

Share that *inferring* is taking background knowledge and adding clues from the text to it in order to figure something out.

Sophie and the rest of you knew that the candy didn't just disappear into thin air. She ate the candy because, like Sophie says, that is what you do with candy. *Inferring* is taking your background knowledge, your BK, and adding clues from the text to figure something out. *[I point to the chart, where it says Bought me some candy/Ain't got it no more.]* Those words are clues about what happened to the candy. I'm going to write the word *clue* next to those words. I took the clue and added my BK to infer what happened to the candy. Sophie, come up here for a minute. *[Sophie comes up. I cup my hands around her ear, whisper, and ask her to say, "I infer that she ate the candy."]*

Sophie: I infer that she ate the candy.

Did you all hear what Sophie said? Turn to each other and talk. What word did Sophie use that is new to us today? *[Kids turn and talk.]*

Jesse: Infer. She said, "I infer."

Exactly. That means Sophie figures that the person in the poem ate the candy. It isn't a guess. We infer that she ate the candy because of the clues in the poem and what we know about what we do with candy. I am going to write *I infer* on the board so that we remember the word and what it means.

Sophie, may I quote you?

Sophie: Yes!

Place Post-its of inferences on a chart of the poem.

I am going to mark this Post-it with an *I* for *infer*. On this Post-it, I am going to quote Sophie and write *She ate the candy* and draw some candy, and then I will put this Post-it up on the chart next to where we can infer that information.

Guide

Let's all read the next part. *[We read the second stanza chorally.]* Let's find the clues in this part that will help us infer what is going on:

Went to the beach

Played on the shore

Built me a sandhouse

Ain't got it no more

Ain't got it no more

So she was at the beach. That is a clue. What did she do there?

Jackson: Built a sandhouse. It's like a sand castle.

I agree. And just like the candy, it's gone now. Let's try something. I have this thinksheet for each of you that says *I infer* right on the top. *[I hand out pencils and clipboards with copies of the* I Infer *Thinksheet.]* I want you to draw what you infer happened to that sandhouse. You may choose a thinksheet that has more lines for writing or one that has more space for drawing, whichever you prefer. *[Kids spread out and spend five to ten minutes drawing what they infer happened to the sandhouse.]*

OK, now share your drawing with a partner and talk about what you infer happened to the sandhouse. *[Kids turn, talk, and share their drawings.]* Who has thoughts about this and would like to share a drawing? This is how to do it. *[I hold up a thinksheet and say, "I infer."]* Who wants to try? *[Several kids share what they infer, holding up their thinksheet.]*

Max: I infer that the water washed the sandhouse away.

Lilly: I infer that a wave washed it away.

Lacey: I infer that someone stepped on it.

Such good inferring. You know that waves can wash away sand castles on the beach. And that someone can step on sand castles and ruin them and then the water washes away what's left. I'm going to write the word *Clue* next to this part of the poem, where it says *Built me a sandhouse/Ain't got it no more.* Those words are a clue about what happened to the sandhouse. We used our BK to infer that the sandhouse disappeared because it was washed away by the waves. Or maybe stepped on. I will write an *I* on this Post-it for *infer,* because you all helped me to infer that the water washed the sandhouse away. I could draw it, too, couldn't I?

Read another section of the poem and invite kids to draw or write what they infer is going on.

Invite kids to share their inferences, first with a partner and then the whole group.

Practice Independently

Read the last section and infer the meaning of it.

Let's look at the last part of the poem. Let's all say it together:

Went to the kitchen
Lay down on the floor
Made me a poem
Still got it
Still got it

What is different about this part?

Rachel: She still has the poem.

Exactly. The candy and the sandhouse disappeared, but she still has the poem. Why? Turn and talk about that. What do you infer? *[Kids turn and talk.]*

Invite kids to jot down or draw what they infer on thinksheets.

OK, now I am going to give you another *I Infer* Thinksheet. *[I offer fresh copies of the* I Infer *Thinksheet.]* Go ahead, find a comfortable spot, spread out on the floor, and jot down or draw what you infer happened at the end of the poem. Remember to think about what you already know and use clues to infer what is going on. *[Kids spend about five or ten minutes drawing what they infer.]*

Share the Learning

Turn to a person next to you and share your thinksheet. Read what you wrote and talk about what you drew. You will share with a partner first, then share with the whole class. *[Kids share with their partners, then prepare to share with the class.]* Who would like to share what they inferred?

> Hannah: The candy was good to eat, but you can't eat poems.
>
> Emily: The poem was so important to her that she kept it.
>
> Jackson: She saves the poem so she can keep it for a long time.

Such great thinking. All of you had very interesting ideas and such great drawings of what you inferred. That poem is really important to her, and she will always have it. When you create a piece of writing, you can keep it forever. The candy and the sandhouse disappear, but the poem stays forever. The poet didn't tell us that. We had to infer it, didn't we? Let's write that on a Post-it for the chart. *[I write and read out loud,* things disappear, but a poem lasts forever *and place the Post-it on the chart.]*

I just thought of something. Maybe that's why Eloise Greenfield called the poem "Things!" I'm not sure, but I am inferring that could be one reason: things disappear, but poems last forever. So cool!

Let's read "Things" one more time. *[We read the poem together from start to finish.]* This sounds so cool. Listen to the rhythm. You are performing the poem, which is more than just reading it. It makes me want to listen! We will keep reading poems from this collection for a few more days, learn some more reading strategies, and have some fun! And if you have some inferences about this poem on Post-its, feel free to place them on the chart later on whenever you have some time.

Invite kids to share their inferences, either orally or with their thinksheets.

Read the poem one last time.

Reflect& Assess

We use poetry to launch inferring because readers almost always have to infer to understand a poem. In addition, most young kids love the sound of poetry. As we teach kids to infer, we teach them the language of inferential thinking. When they say "maybe" or "I think..." they are likely inferring. So we listen intently to their conversations to see when they are thinking inferentially. Just because kids say they are inferring doesn't mean they are. And just because they don't use the term *infer* doesn't mean they are not. When kids say, "I infer...," we need to explore further to see if they are really thinking inferentially. Inferring actually comes quite naturally to young kids. They burst with questions of all types, and frequently, as soon as they ask a question, they begin to infer an answer. So we listen carefully to their questions and attempts to answer them. We label those answers *inferences* when kids merge their background knowledge with clues from the text to come up with something that wasn't explicitly stated.

Adapt& Differentiate

This lesson was done with kindergarteners, but here are suggestions for how to adapt and differentiate for the whole range of learners.

To help kids understand the nature of inferential thinking, we continue to focus on inferring meaning from poetry. Poems are often short and sweet, and kids love them. We create charts of all different types of poems and guide kids to infer in both large and small groups. They listen to the poems and mark the charts with *I* for inference when they infer. They also draw their thinking on the poem Anchor Chart. As kids' thinking develops, we are likely to choose slightly more complex poems, challenging them to rely even more on inferring to understand.

The three *I Infer* Thinksheets used in this lesson differ in how much space they offer for drawing and writing. Kids can choose their paper based on their desire and which best meets their needs. Younger kids often choose the paper with the most space for drawing. More developed readers often want more space for writing. Either works.

Kindergarten Thinksheets

1 Zoe inferred that the poet ate the candy, which is exactly what happened!

I infer... THE

WODr WOSHD

THE SHAND HAVE

4WAU.

2 This student inferred that the water washed the sandhouse away. A reasonable inference that makes sense in the poem.

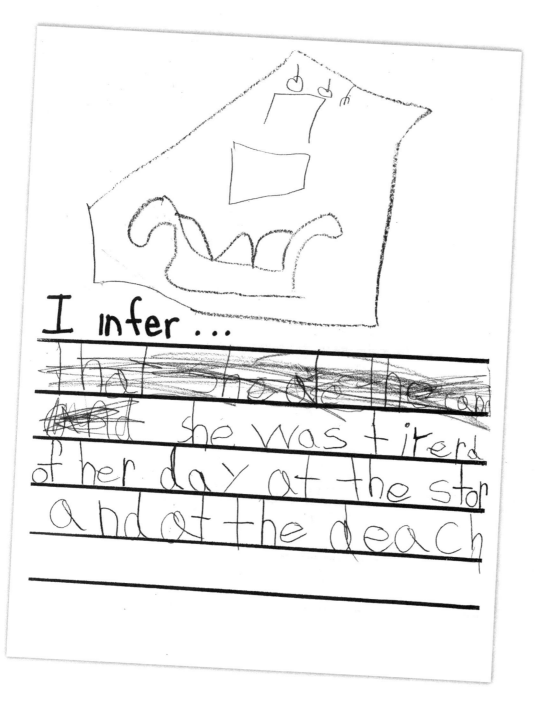

I infer ...

~~[scribbled out line]~~

she was tirerd
of her day at the stor
and at the beach

3 Hallie inferred that the girl in the poem was tired after a long day at the store and at the beach and lay down because of it. The poem indicates that the girl was quite active and then lay down and wrote the poem. Hallie is activating her background knowledge about such a day. It's reasonable to infer that the person was tired! I would meet with Hallie to talk about what else we might be able to infer from the clues. Sometimes readers rely too much on their background knowledge to make an inference. They need to consider the text clues as well.

"A poem like Honey, I Love. I just love Honey, I Love. The sandhouse was better than the candy. I love building sandhouses. I really do."

4 This student chose a thinksheet with a lot of space to write—and write he did! He wrote about how much he loves the poem, stated that the sandhouse is better than the candy, and wrote about how much he likes building sand-houses. Rather than infer the meaning of the poem, the student connected the poem to his own experience, which is a wonderful thing to do. I would confer with him to celebrate his writing and his background knowledge. Then we could talk about what he might infer and explore that a bit.

ALEX

I infer... THE
POLLUM WUS THE
in. portnis uv
DLL

5 Alex said it in a nutshell. He inferred that the poem was the most important of all!

Lesson (12) Guide

This Lesson Guide can help you teach students to merge their background knowledge with the text to draw reasonable and helpful inferences using any text of your choice.

Infer Meaning

Merge background knowledge with clues from the text

TEACHING MOVES	TEACHING LANGUAGE

Connect and Engage

Share the cover of the book and flip through the poems, explaining that the book is a collection of poems by one author.	▪ I brought this wonderful book of poems. It's a collection of poems by....
Have kids turn and talk about what they know about poetry.	▪ Turn and talk to each other about what you know about poetry.
	▪ What are some of the things you already know about poetry? Good noticing. Say more about that.... What makes you think that?
Read the poem aloud rhythmically.	▪ I selected this poem called...from the collection and wrote it on a chart so you can all see. Let me read it for you. Listen to the rhythm.
Read the poem together, with kids echoing the lines as you say them.	▪ Let's try it together. Let's say it as though you are the echo. I say the line first and then you say the line.

Model

Explain that readers often have to infer the meaning of poetry to understand it.	▪ Sometimes poetry doesn't give you all of the information; you have to figure it out. We call that *inferring*.
	▪ For instance, I have a question. What happened when.... You may know the answer, but the poem doesn't tell us exactly. You have to infer.
Share that *inferring* is taking background knowledge and adding clues from the text to it in order to figure something out.	▪ Inferring is taking your background knowledge and adding clues from the text to figure something out. The words in this poem are clues about.... I paid attention to the clues and then added my background knowledge to figure out what was happening—to infer meaning. I'm going to write *clue* next to these words on the chart.
	▪ I am going to ask one of you to say this sentence: "I infer that...." What word is new to us today? I am going to write *infer* on the board so we remember it.
Place Post-its of inferences on a chart of the poem.	▪ I'm going to put Post-its of my inferences up on the chart right next to where we inferred.

The Teaching Moves outline your instructional sequence and the
Teaching Language gives you an idea about what to say to your students.

TEACHING LANGUAGE	TEACHING MOVES

Guide

- Let's all read the next part and find clues that will help us infer what is going on.

- Choose a thinksheet that has more lines for writing or more space for drawing, whichever you prefer. On the thinksheet, draw what you infer is going on here....

Read another section of the poem and invite kids to draw or write what they infer is going on.

- Now share your drawing with a partner and talk about what you infer....Who would like to hold up your thinksheet, like this, and share?

Invite kids to share their inferences, first with a partner and then the whole group.

Practice Independently

- Let's look at the last part of the poem and say it together. Now turn and talk about that. What do you infer?

Read the last section and infer the meaning of it.

- On this new thinksheet, jot down or draw what you infer is going on.

Invite kids to jot down or draw what they infer on thinksheets.

Share the Learning

- Turn to a partner and share your thinksheet. Read what you wrote and talk about what you drew.

- Who would like to share what they inferred?

Invite kids to share their inferences, either orally or with their thinksheets.

- Let's read the poem one more time. Listen to the rhythm. You are performing the poem, which is more than just reading it.

Read the poem one last time.

Reflect & Assess

Did your students:

- understand what it means to infer?
- infer the meaning of poems by merging their background knowledge with clues from the text?
- grow to cherish the sound of words and the rhythm of language?

Text Matters

In this lesson and the previous one, we use poetry to teach comprehension to young learners. When showing younger kids how to infer and visualize, poetry is a great genre with which to begin. Poems are short, patterned, and fun to savor aloud. Poetry, by its very nature, leaves a lot to the imagination. The poet leaves clues in the poem, and readers must merge those clues with their background knowledge to make meaning. Poets paint pictures with their words, which causes the reader to visualize. When launching inferring and visualizing, we choose poetry that kids can relate to, so that they can use their background knowledge to help them understand. For this lesson, we especially look for poems with sections kids can act out physically. And as we often do, we choose poems that are fun and rhythmic, so kids enjoy them.

Resources & Materials

Lesson Text

Honey, I Love and other love poems by Eloise Greenfield (HarperCollins Publishers, 1978) [Available in the Trade Book Pack.]

Classroom Supplies
- "Rope Rhyme" Anchor Chart
- "Honey, I Love" Anchor Chart

Student Supplies
- Drawing paper
- Assorted markers, pencils, and crayons

Get a picture in your mind

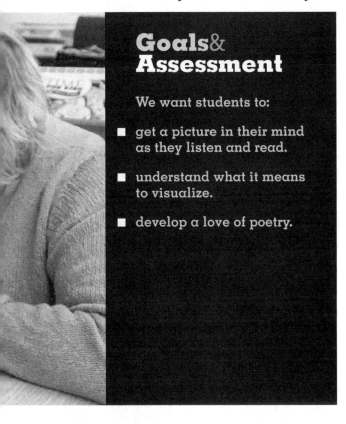

Goals& Assessment

We want students to:

- get a picture in their mind as they listen and read.

- understand what it means to visualize.

- develop a love of poetry.

How

Connect and Engage

- Read a poem and ask kids to infer what it is about.

Model

- Explain that readers get pictures in their minds when they are listening or reading and that this is called *visualizing*.

- Share a well-known story and think aloud about what you visualize. Then ask kids to share what they picture in their minds.

- Share what you visualize as you read the poem aloud and ask kids what they visualize.

- Invite kids to act out what they visualize.

Guide

- Read another poem in sections or stanzas and have kids talk about what they visualize.

Practice Independently

- Invite kids to draw what they visualize from the poem.

Share the Learning

- Invite kids to the sharing circle to talk about their drawing and what they visualized.

- Remind kids what *inferring* is.

- Explore how visualizing and inferring are related.

Why& What

Visualizing is sort of a first cousin to inferring. When we visualize, we are really inferring with a picture in our minds. When readers visualize, they construct meaning by creating sensory images, not only picturing the words but also hearing, smelling, and tasting them. Younger children are particularly inclined to visualize as they listen to and read stories, often living through or living in the stories. Poetry is an ideal genre to introduce visualizing as well as inferring. We gain a deeper understanding of poetry when we create sensory images as we read. And we enjoy our reading and listening more fully when we visualize in this way.

HONEY, I LOVE
and other love poems
by Eloise Greenfield
pictures by Diane and Leo Dillon
25th ANNIVERSARY

READING RAINBOW BOOK

Lesson Text

I chose to stay with Eloise Greenfield's *Honey, I Love and other love poems* to launch visualizing. Greenfield paints vivid pictures with the words she writes. It is almost impossible for kids not to get mental images as they listen to and read poems from this collection. When we teach visualizing, kids must be able to activate their background knowledge to help them to create mental images. I added "Rope Rhyme" and "Honey I Love" to teach visualizing, because most kids can connect to something in these two poems. They have some background knowledge for the events and ideas that Greenfield writes about. In fact, kids can relate to almost every poem in this collection, which makes it a great text for teaching both visualizing and inferring. The poems themselves are so much fun to read and listen to that kids end up saying them over and over again, just because they love them.

From *Honey, I Love and other love poems*, by Eloise Greenfield. Text copyright © 1978 by Eloise Greenfield. Used by permission of HarperCollins Publishers.

TEACHING MOVES   **TEACHING LANGUAGE**

Connect and Engage

Read a poem and ask kids to infer what it is about.

We are going to spend some more time today inferring with poetry, and we are going to learn another strategy. I am going to start by reading another poem by Eloise Greenfield that I have written on a chart, but I am not going to tell you the title. Listen carefully and think about your BK, your background knowledge. I want you to infer what is going on in the poem. *[I read "Rope Rhyme" rhythmically, without revealing the title.]*

   Turn to each other and talk. What do you infer is going on in this poem? *[Kids turn and talk, and I crouch down and listen in.]* So what is she doing?

   All: Jumping rope!

   Exactly. Eloise Greenfield didn't tell us—we had to infer that the girl is jumping rope. What are some clues that led you to believe that she is jumping rope? *[Kids share some of the phrases, such as* "listen to the rope when it hits the ground, jump right in," *and* "jump right out."*]*

   Now I am going to let you in on a secret. I am going to write the title of this poem at the top. It is called "Rope Rhyme"

Rope Rhyme

Get set, ready now, jump right in
Bounce and kick and giggle and spin
Listen to the rope when it hits the ground
Listen to that clappedy-clappedy sound
Jump right up when it tells you to
Come back down, whatever you do
Count to a hundred, count by ten
Start to count all over again
That's what jumping is all about
Get set, ready now,
                  jump
                      right
                          out!

because it *is* about jumping rope, just like you inferred. Let's read "Rope Rhyme" together with echoes and with rhythm. *[We read "Rope Rhyme" with me leading and kids echoing.]* There you go again! Sounds like a performance. You are all performance poets! So cool.

Model

Lately, we have been talking about inferring, but readers do other things besides infer when they read. Sometimes when readers read and think about what they are reading, they get pictures in their minds. We call that *visualizing*. Visualizing is like seeing a movie in your mind. When I read *The Three Bears*, I get a picture in my mind. I see the bears. The papa is really big, the mama is medium size, and the baby bear is little. They are all brown, at least in my mind they are. I suppose they could be black, but I have this picture in my mind and they are brown. That's what visualizing is. You all know the story of *The Three Bears*, right? *[All nod.]* Think about *The Three Bears* for a minute. Think about where they live and about Goldilocks and what happens to her. Can you picture Goldilocks in your mind? What does she look like? Turn to each other and talk. *[Kids turn and talk about Goldilocks's long, blond hair, her dress, etc. I crouch down to listen.]* As I listen to you, it seems you all have a picture of Goldilocks with long, blond hair, but some of you said her dress is red and others said it is white. That is because we each get a different picture in our mind. Think about the inside of the Bears' house. What do you see in there? *[Responses include:]*

> Three chairs, one all broken.
>
> Goldilocks sleeping in Baby Bear's bed.
>
> A house in the woods.

So, some of you saw the chairs, others the bed, and still others the cottage in the woods. Some saw the outside, and some of you were picturing the inside of the cottage. That's *visualizing*: getting a picture in your mind.

Let's read "Rope Rhyme" again and see what we visualize. *[I read the poem from the Anchor Chart.]*

When I read "Rope Rhyme," I visualize when I was in grade school jumping rope on the playground with my friends. Two kids are twirling the rope, and I am jumping double with my best friend, Mary Ann. Close your eyes and visualize yourself in this poem. Where are you? What are you doing? Turn to each other and talk. *[Kids turn and talk.]*

> Brianna: I'm on the playground jumping rope with friends.
>
> Jason: I don't jump rope. I'm playing soccer.

That makes sense, Jason, but did you ever see anyone jump rope? If so, what did it look like?

> Jason: Kids swinging the rope and jumping.

Explain that readers get pictures in their minds when they are listening or reading and that this is called *visualizing*.

Share a well-known story and think aloud about what you visualize. Then ask kids to share what they picture in their minds.

Share what you visualize as you read the poem aloud and ask kids what they visualize.

Exactly. You can visualize something even if you have never done it, can't you? That's visualizing: getting an image or a picture in your mind of the words you hear in the poem. Most of you were visualizing jumping rope or watching someone jump rope, but you were in different places and wearing different clothes. The poet leaves that part up to you.

Brenda: When I was visualizing the poem, I could hear the rope slapping the ground, too.

You could *hear* the poem, too, Brenda. Fantastic! Sometimes when we really start visualizing, we can even hear, or smell, or taste things in the poem. Isn't that something?

Who wants to come up here and act out what you visualized in "Rope Rhyme"? Devon and Sophie, come on up. *[We huddle, plan our action, and then Devon and I twirl an imaginary rope while Sophie jumps in and keeps jumping.]* What are we doing?

All: Jumping rope.

It's kind of like what we visualized while we were listening to the poem, isn't it? *[Kids nod.]* We do a lot of visualizing when we read and listen. Visualizing makes us want to read and hear more. Everyone stand up and act out what you visualized in "Rope Rhyme." *[Kids jump up and down gleefully.]* This is so much fun!

Guide

Let's take a look at another poem in this collection. I have written it on another chart. Let's read "Honey, I Love." I'll point to each part as I read it. You can echo it, read with me, or just listen, whatever you prefer. *[I read the first page of "Honey, I Love."]* Turn to each other and talk about what you visualized. *[Kids turn and talk as I crouch down and listen in.]* So, what pictures did you have in your mind? *[Responses include:]*

Her cousin is coming over.

He was whistling.

They got all wet in the hose.

Lots of kids are playing in the water, having fun.

So interesting. The writer didn't say the people were having fun, but you got a picture of them playing and having fun, which makes a lot of sense. Let's read on. *[I read the second page and have kids turn and talk about what they visualize. Then I read the third page and ask kids to turn and talk again about what they visualize. They share a range of things they visualize: riding in a car, playing with dolls, loving mom, and not loving going to sleep.]*

This is so cool. The pictures in your mind are different from one another because we are all different! We don't all visualize the same image, which makes it interesting when we get together and talk with each other about stories or poems.

Invite kids to act out what they visualize.

TIP: Young kids need to move, and poetry offers a terrific opportunity for movement. The rhythm of poetry just begs kids to get up, move around, and act out the poem. Find as many possibilities for drama and movement as you can with young kids. When we make the text physical, young learners will engage more completely and understand and remember more.

Read another poem in sections or stanzas and have kids talk about what they visualize.

HONEY, I LOVE

I love
I love a lot of things, a whole lot of things
Like
My cousin comes to visit and you know he's from the South
'Cause every word he says just kind of slides out of his mouth
I like the way he whistles and I like the way he walks
But honey, let me tell you that I LOVE the way he talks
    I love the way my cousin talks
            and

The day is hot and icky and the sun sticks to my skin
Mr. Davis turns the hose on, everybody jumps right in
The water stings my stomach, and I feel so nice and cool
Honey, let me tell you that I LOVE a flying pool
    I love to feel a flying pool
            and

Renee comes out to play and brings her doll without a dress
I make a dress with paper and that doll sure looks a mess
We laugh so loud and long and hard the doll falls to the ground
Honey, let me tell you that I LOVE the laughing sound
    I love to make the laughing sound
            and

My uncle's car is crowded and there's lots of food to eat
We're going down the country where the church folks like to meet
I'm looking out the window at the cows and trees outside
Honey, let me tell you that I LOVE to take a ride
    I love to take a family ride
            and

My mama's on the sofa sewing buttons on my coat
I go and sit beside her, I'm through playing with my boat
I hold her arm and kiss it 'cause it feels so soft and warm
Honey, let me tell you that I LOVE my mama's arm
    I love to kiss my mama's arm
            and

It's not so late at night, but still I'm lying in my bed
I guess I need my rest, at least that's what my mama said
She told me not to cry 'cause she don't want to hear a peep
Honey, let me tell you I DON'T love to go to sleep
    I do not love to go to sleep
But I love
I love a lot of things, a whole lot of things
And honey,
I love you, too.

Practice Independently

Invite kids to draw what they visualize from the poem.

OK, now you get to be an artist. I am going to give you a piece of paper to draw what you visualize from "Honey, I Love," the poem we just read. *[I hand out paper and markers, pencils, and crayons.]* It is on the chart for you to look at. You can pick any part you want and draw what you visualize in that particular part. You can choose the part about the cousin, the part about the hose, the doll, or any part. It's up to you. Draw the pictures you have in your mind and the details you see. In other words, you are going to draw what you visualize. The pictures you get in your mind when you read and hear the poem. Happy drawing! *[Kids draw what they visualize from the poem.]*

Share the Learning

Invite kids to the sharing circle to talk about their drawing and what they visualized.

[Kids share their diverse and fun drawings and talk about what they visualized.] You all did a great job of visualizing. Remind me, what is visualizing exactly? Turn to someone next to you and talk about it. *[Kids turn and talk.]* Who has an idea? Lilly?

Lilly: Getting a picture in your mind.

That's right, visualizing is getting a picture in your mind from the words, getting a mental image of the words. So we might imagine someone jumping rope when we read "Rope Rhyme" or playing in the water from the hose when we read "Honey, I Love."

Remind kids what inferring is.

Now think back to the poem "Things" that we read earlier *[see Lesson 12]*. We learned to infer. What is *inferring?* Turn to each other and talk. *[Kids turn to someone next to them and talk.]*

Jeremiah: Inferring is when you figure something out.

Say more about that, Jeremiah. Give me an example from one of the poems we read.

Jeremiah: Like the candy disappeared in that one poem, because she ate it.

Exactly, that is what it is to *infer.* The writer didn't say what happened to the candy. You had to figure it out. You take the clues in the text and think about what you already know, your BK, to figure something out in the poem or story.

Explore how visualizing and inferring are related.

In some ways, visualizing and inferring are alike. We sometimes think of them as cousins. Because really when you visualize, you are kind of inferring with a picture in your mind. When that candy was gone, what did you visualize?

Jackson: The kid eating it.

So thoughtful, Jackson. You had a picture in your mind of the kid in the poem eating the candy. This collection of poetry by Eloise Greenfield is a great place to practice inferring and visualizing. It has a lot of poems, and we can infer and visualize with every one of them. We can keep paging through these poems, reading through them, thinking about them, acting them out, visualizing, and inferring. And I bet we will have some connections and questions, too. That's what reading is all about. So much fun! I love poetry—the meaning of the words and the sound of them, too!

Did your students:

- get a picture in their mind as they listened and read?

- understand what it means to visualize?

- develop a love of poetry?

Reflect& Assess

There is nothing more fun than teaching young kids to visualize. Most of them are naturally visual, because they have been making sense of the world visually since birth. We continue to encourage kids to close their eyes and picture the story in their minds as we focus on the visualizing strategy. Surrounding young kids with poetry nudges them to visualize. We share poems frequently as we teach visualizing and ask kids to draw the pictures that they have in their minds. It is important to keep in mind that when we assess kids' visualizing, we are not looking for the best rendering in the class. We are looking at their drawings as a window into their thinking. We expect all of the drawings to look different. We are not asking them to draw their favorite parts but rather to draw what they visualized in certain parts of the text, to draw the images the text conjured in their minds as they listened to it.

Adapt& Differentiate

This lesson was done with kindergarteners, but here are suggestions for how to adapt and differentiate for the whole range of learners.

We asked kindergarteners simply to draw what they visualized. Some do elaborate drawings with much detail. Others do less detailed drawings. We need to keep in mind that although details are helpful when constructing meaning, something as simple as a smile or a frown can convey meaning. We model this for kids, showing them how we draw expressions that convey meaning. Some kindergarteners naturally add words, labels, and phrases to their pictures. We model this particularly for first and second graders. The drawings of older first and second graders are generally more detailed and often include more writing.

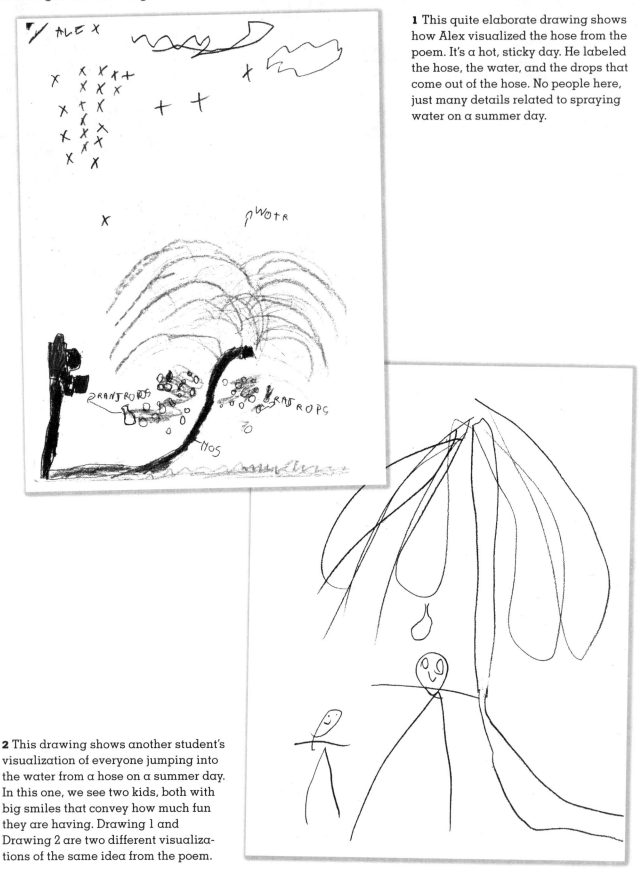

1 This quite elaborate drawing shows how Alex visualized the hose from the poem. It's a hot, sticky day. He labeled the hose, the water, and the drops that come out of the hose. No people here, just many details related to spraying water on a summer day.

2 This drawing shows another student's visualization of everyone jumping into the water from a hose on a summer day. In this one, we see two kids, both with big smiles that convey how much fun they are having. Drawing 1 and Drawing 2 are two different visualizations of the same idea from the poem.

3 This drawing shows the girl in the poem playing with a doll without a dress. The girl has clothes on, but the doll is undressed, just as in the poem.

4 Hallie drew what she visualized about the uncle's car on a country drive. She included the crowded car and someone looking out the window at the trees and the cows, just as described in the poem.

5 Lilly visualized the part of the poem in which the girl doesn't love to go to sleep. She has included the thought, "Get me out of here!" It is a good example of how strategies interact. Lilly visualizes herself not wanting to go to bed.

Learn to Visualize

Get a picture in your mind

TEACHING MOVES	TEACHING LANGUAGE
	Connect and Engage
Read a poem and ask kids to infer what it is about.	■ I am going to read you a poem by…but I'm not going to tell you the title. Listen carefully and think about your background knowledge. I want you to infer what is going on in the poem.
	■ Turn to each other and talk. What do you infer is going on in this poem?
	■ Now let's look at the title. How does it compare to our inferences?
	Model
Explain that readers get pictures in their minds when they are listening or reading and that this is called *visualizing*.	■ When readers read and think about what they are reading, they get pictures in their minds. We call that *visualizing*.
Share a well-known story and think aloud about what you visualize. Then ask kids to share what they picture in their minds.	■ Think about the story of *The Three Bears* for a minute. Get a picture in your mind of where they live and Goldilocks and what happens to her. Turn and talk about that.
	■ Some of you saw Goldilocks's long, blond hair, others the chairs, and still others the bed. That is because we all get different pictures in our minds. That's visualizing: getting a picture in your mind.
Share what you visualize as you read the poem aloud and ask kids what they visualize.	■ Let's read…again and see what we visualize. I visualize…. Close your eyes and visualize yourself in this poem. Now turn to each other and talk. Where are you? What are you doing?
Invite kids to act out what they visualize.	■ Who wants to come up and act out what you visualized in this poem?
	Guide
Read another poem in sections or stanzas and have kids talk about what they visualize.	■ Let's read the poem I have written on this Anchor Chart. You can echo it, read with me, or just listen, whichever you prefer.
	■ Turn to each other and talk. What pictures are you getting in your mind?

The Teaching Moves outline your instructional sequence and the
Teaching Language gives you an idea about what to say to your students.

TEACHING LANGUAGE	TEACHING MOVES
Practice Independently	
▪ I am going to give you some paper and markers to draw what you visualize from the poem. It is on the Anchor Chart for you to look at.	Invite kids to draw what they visualize from the poem.
Share the Learning	
▪ Now that you are all here together, turn and talk about what you drew and visualized.	Invite kids to the sharing circle to talk about their drawing and what they visualized.
▪ Think back to the poem…where we learned to infer. Turn to each other and talk about what inferring is.	Remind kids what *inferring* is.
▪ Visualizing and inferring are alike so we sometimes think of them as cousins. When you visualize, you are inferring with a picture in your mind.	Explore how visualizing and inferring are related.
▪ Poetry is a great way to practice visualizing and inferring. When we read poems, we visualize and infer. We also are likely to have a lot of connections and questions. I love poetry, the meaning of the words and the sound of them, too!	

**Reflect&
Assess**

Did your students:

- ▪ get a picture in their mind as they listened and read?
- ▪ understand what it means to visualize?
- ▪ develop a love of poetry?

Make Sense of New Information

Text Matters

Visualizing and inferring are sometimes seen as more useful for understanding stories and narratives than for understanding nonfiction. Yet many nonfiction texts invite kids to create mind pictures and inferences, which helps them to better understand information. Texts that invite inferential thinking burst with features including diagrams, photographs, labels, captions, maps, headings, and bold print. We work to keep kids' visualizations and inferences tied to the text features and pictures, discouraging them from making wild guesses and supporting them to make reasonable inferences that fill in what the text doesn't say. When choosing informational text for inferring and visualizing, we look for books with great cover photographs and make sure that the interior pictures and words spark a wide variety of inferences.

Resources&Materials

Lesson Text
TIME For Kids Bigger Picture Edition [April 2005] "Ladybugs Grow Up" poster

Additional Texts
- Nonfiction texts on various topics with clear photographs and a range of visual and text features

Classroom Supplies
- Post-its
- Clipboards
- Pencils

Student Supplies
- Student copy of "Ladybugs Grow Up" [See *Keep Reading! A Source Book of Short Text*, pages 9–12, or the DVD-ROM.]
- Clipboard with pencil and Post-its or Post-its Thinksheets [See *Strategy Book 4*, pages 70-71, or the DVD-ROM.]

Infer from features, pictures, and words

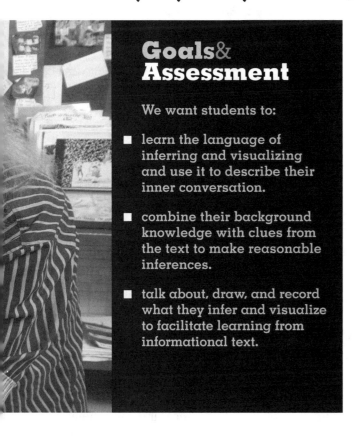

Goals& Assessment

We want students to:

- **learn the language of inferring and visualizing and use it to describe their inner conversation.**

- **combine their background knowledge with clues from the text to make reasonable inferences.**

- **talk about, draw, and record what they infer and visualize to facilitate learning from informational text.**

Why&What

Often kids do not realize that they naturally use their experiences and background knowledge to infer information from pictures and text. This lesson shows them how to combine what they already know with information from images, words, and features to better understand the material. When kids understand the power of their own thinking as they make sense of information, their enthusiasm for learning soars. We encourage kids to share inferences and mind pictures by drawing and writing what they are visualizing and inferring. In this lesson we build on the vocabulary of visualizing and inferring, encouraging kids to use language such as "I think," "Maybe," "I visualize," and "I infer." We illustrate inferring with a picture equation that makes the process as concrete as possible for kids.

How

Connect and Engage

- Share inferences and elicit kids' thinking about the cover photograph.
- Teach and draw the inference equation.
- Ask kids to turn and talk about the features they notice.

Model

- Show kids how we infer, combining background knowledge with clues from the words and photos to make meaning.
- Have kids turn and talk about photos and features using the phrases "I think," "I infer," and "I visualize."
- Use an example from a child to demonstrate how to make an inference.
- Show how to infer the meaning of an unfamiliar word and mark a Post-it with an *I* for *inference.*

Guide

- Invite kids to turn and talk and then share their inferences.
- Encourage kids to notice features and text that demonstrate sequence.
- Reiterate the language of inferring and visualizing and tie it to the features.

Practice Independently

- Invite kids to write down and/or draw their inferences, saying "I think," "I infer," or "I visualize."

Share the Learning

- Encourage kids to share their learning—using the language of visualizing and inferring.
- Wrap up the lesson by asking kids to put their Post-its up for all to see.

Lesson Text

The *TIME For Kids* Bigger Picture Edition "Ladybugs Grow Up" poster is chock-full of photographs, features, and information that encourage kids to create mind pictures and infer. Kids infer information based on the text and features, especially the sequence of photos of the ladybug life cycle that explain the growth and development of these insects. In science text like this, photographs and other features often help kids infer the meaning of words like *larva* and *pupa*, so that they learn unfamiliar vocabulary by using the context.

Used with permission from *Time For Kids*.

TEACHING MOVES	TEACHING LANGUAGE

Connect and Engage

Share inferences and elicit kids' thinking about the cover photograph.

Let's take a look at this incredible photograph of ladybugs on the cover. *[I show the front of* TIME For Kids *"Ladybugs Grow Up" poster.]* Listen to the title of the article: "Ladybugs Grow Up." When I think about the title and the photo, I *infer* from the words "grow up" that the article is going to be about how ladybugs develop from eggs into adult insects. I know they start their life as eggs, and we see some of these eggs up in the corner. *[I point to eggs in the picture.]* I use my background knowledge to understand clues, such as the eggs in the photograph and the words "Bugs in Eggs."

OK now, look carefully at this photograph, then turn and talk about something you infer or think about it. You might start your thought with "I infer" or "I think."

> Adolpho: I think that ladybug is eating the green bug! Right there!
>
> Frankie: I infer the eggs are tiny.
>
> Briana: I think when the ladybugs hatch out of their eggs, they have no spots and then they get spots.

TIP: With young children, instead of "inference equation," we would use simpler language, such as "number sentence," to describe how we can combine text clues and background knowledge to make an inference.

This is such great thinking! Some of you used the phrase "I think" or "I infer" when you inferred from the photograph. When you say these phrases, you are using your background knowledge and thinking about the pictures and text to make meaning. Maybe the words and pictures don't tell you all you need to know, so you have to add your own thinking.

Teach and draw the inference equation.

Now I'm going to draw a picture so that we'll remember what to do when we infer. We'll call it the "inference equation." It's a number sentence like $2 + 2 = 4$.

[I draw an open book that has pictures and words on the pages and a person with a brain, explaining as I draw.] So, we have clues from the text—that's my picture of a book that has pictures and words on the page. And we combine text clues with our background knowledge—I'll show our background knowledge by drawing a person with a brain! We combine clues from the text and our background knowledge to make an inference. So, this is the inference equation.

pictures and words ↓

background knowledge ↓

= an inference

text clues   what we know

[I open to the inside page spread.] Turn and talk about some of the features you notice on this page. You already know that we can learn a lot of information from visual and text features, so let's share what some of them are. *[Kids share features they notice: captions, labels, arrows, photos, and close-ups.]* That's a great list. Now we'll begin reading and learning from those features!

Ask kids to turn and talk about the features they notice.

Model

I'm going to read the words, images, and features in our poster. Watch how I use the phrases "I think" and "I infer" to combine what I know with clues from the photographs, features, and text. That's what thoughtful readers do!

Show kids how we infer, combining background knowledge with clues from the words and photos to make meaning.

A Ladybug's Life

That's the title. *[I continue reading.]*

The life cycle of a ladybug begins in the spring. A ladybug passes through three stages. Then it becomes an adult beetle.

I'm inferring that these are photographs of the three stages the ladybug goes through as it grows up. The photos are in order: the ladybug is first an egg, right here in Picture 1. Then we see a larva in Picture 2, which shows what the next stage of the life cycle looks like. And then the ladybug becomes a pupa, right here in Picture 3. The ladybug grows and develops into an adult ladybug, which you see in Picture 4. The numbers—1, 2, 3, and 4—show a sequence. A sequence is when we put things in order—first, second, third, and so on. The photos tell me what the ladybug looks like during each stage in its life cycle. I think the captions next to each photo probably describe what happens at each stage.

So take a moment to look at the photographs and features on this page. As you turn and talk, try to use the words "I think," or "I infer," or "I visualize."

Have kids turn and talk about photos and features using the phrases "I think," "I infer," and "I visualize."

Briana: At the bottom, there are labels. I think they tell us the parts of the ladybug.

Adolpho: I think that picture by the number 2 looks like an alligator.

You are such careful observers—that's what scientists do: They look carefully and learn from what they notice. You are inferring information using the features.

Use an example from a
child to demonstrate how to
make an inference.

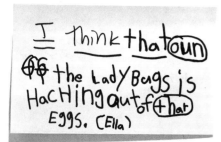

Show how to infer the
meaning of an unfamiliar
word and mark a Post-it
with an *I* for inference.

TIP: We teach kids to mark the
text with codes for different
strategies—a star or * (asterisk)
for important information, a *?*
for a question, an *I* for an
inference. When kids code their
thinking in this way, they are
demonstrating their use of
thinking strategies.

I'm going to read a bit—let's see. I think I'll start with the caption next to the number 1, that's the first stage in the ladybug's life cycle.

> *A female ladybug finds a leaf. It lays hundreds of eggs. The tiny oval eggs stay close together.*

Ella: I think that one of the ladybugs is hatching out of the eggs.

How thoughtful, Ella. The caption didn't tell us that the ladybug is coming out of the egg. You inferred what is happening from the photo. I think your inference is right on! Would you be willing to write your thought on a Post-it, Ella? Then we'll put it on the article. We'll keep reading to see if we can confirm Ella's inference.

> *After a few days, the eggs hatch. Out come little bugs that look like alligators.*

That's what you inferred, Ella. So you were right on! And Adolpho, the author of this article described the larva as an alligator, which is just what you said! I'll keep reading...

> *Each is called a larva. It eats many aphids and gets big.*

I wasn't sure what the word *larva* meant, but I inferred the meaning from the words and pictures here. I learned that a larva is the next stage in a ladybug's life cycle—after the egg—and that larva are little bugs that hatch out of the eggs. I'm going to write on a Post-it: *The larva are little bugs that come out of the eggs. It's the second stage of the ladybug life cycle.* I'll mark my Post-it with an *I* to show I was making an inference.

The larva are little bugs that come out of the eggs. It's the second stage of the ladybug life cycle.

Guide

Invite kids to turn and talk
and then share their
inferences.

Encourage kids to notice
features and text that
demonstrate sequence.

Now it's your turn. Remember our number sentence about inferring? It's when we combine our background knowledge with the words and features to make meaning. Take a look at the features, think about what you know, and then turn and talk to someone about what you infer. *[As the kids talk, I listen in to conversations and confer with kids, looking for kids whom I will invite to share out their thinking with the large group.]*

OK, let's share out some of your thinking. Ansel, you noticed something really interesting about the numbers. Please share.

Ansel: In math, we started with 1 when we were putting things in a sequence. Here there's 1, 2, 3, and 4.

Yes, Ansel. Putting things in a sequence means you are putting them in order. We know to read the number 1 picture first, then the number 2 picture and caption, and so on. The order is important, and the numbers show us the stages of the ladybug's life cycle: the egg, the larva, the pupa, and finally the adult ladybug.

Zoe: The arrows tell that the ladybug is changing.

Zoe, you inferred a big idea. You looked at the arrows and inferred the idea that the ladybug changes and develops into an adult ladybug. We infer from visual features, such as photographs, and text features, such as captions, that tell us how the ladybug is changing as it grows up.

> **Reiterate the language of inferring and visualizing and tie it to the features.**

Ian: I think it's eating the bugs on the plant in the photo.

Tell us more about your thinking, please, Ian.

Ian: Look, it's those green bugs. The larva is eating those aphids up! I can visualize the larva growing and growing!

Thanks for explaining that food is important to the ladybug as it grows up, Ian. Notice the language that Ian used. Ian's description of what he inferred and visualized helped me create a picture in my mind. From your words, Ian, we can all visualize that larva getting bigger and bigger as it gobbles up those aphids.

Practice Independently

[I hand out clipboards with paper and pencil and Post-its or copies of the Six-Up Post-its *Thinksheet.]* I want you all to draw or write your thinking on Post-its as you read your own text. You can use your copy of the ladybug text or choose a non-fiction book from the baskets. Remember to combine what you know with what you are learning from the features and words and use the inferring language: "I think," "I infer," and "I visualize."

> **Invite kids to write down and/or draw their inferences, saying "I think," "I infer," or "I visualize."**

[I confer with Jeannie who is reading the Ladybug TFK *poster.]*

The larva sheds its skin a few times over the next two to three weeks. A new, hard skin grows, and the ladybug turns into a pupa.

Jeannie: I infer that, after a few weeks, it will turn into a ladybug.

Yes, Jeannie, you are inferring what is going to happen next. Maybe you have a picture of that ladybug in your mind. Try to draw or write that on your Post-it.

Jeannie: I can see that ladybugs look really different when they grow up. I'm amazed that the pupa turns into a ladybug!

Yes, they look very different than they did in the earlier stages of the life cycle. You can show your thinking by drawing what you just explained.

> **TIP:** It is often easier for young children to draw their thinking rather than trying to write it down, so I encourage this.

Share the Learning

Encourage kids to share their learning—using the language of visualizing and inferring.

TIP: Kids gather in a sharing circle with materials on the floor in front of them so they are not constantly rustling, waving, or getting distracted by their own materials while listening to a classmate who is sharing. We ask kids to keep their own papers on the rug unless they are actually sharing with the group.

TIP: A ritual like the sharing circle has several benefits. It enables kids to run the sharing on their own. It encourages kids to speak to their classmates rather than directing everything to the teacher. In addition, after kids share, they ask the group, "Any questions or comments?" inviting kids to extend their thinking beyond the "I liked how you…" refrain. With this prompt, kids learn to ask appropriate questions or offer a comment that elaborates on the information shared.

Wrap up the lesson by asking kids to put their Post-its up for all to see.

[Kids gather in the sharing circle, putting their articles and Post-its on the floor in front of them. They call on each other, asking, "Would you like to share?" The child whose turn it is to share replies, "Yes, thank you."]

OK, who would like to share? I'll get the share started, and then you can run it yourselves. Will you start, Michelle? I'll say, "Michelle, would you like to share?"

Michelle: Yes, thank you. I did a picture. The ladybug is looking for food. I infer she is hungry. I drew a picture of the ladybug, all grown up! Any questions or comments?

Zoe: I learned from your picture that the ladybug was looking for food— you visualized that.

Zoe, you learned from Michelle about what the ladybug was doing. And, Michelle, you looked carefully at the picture of a ladybug eating aphids and made a reasonable inference.

[Michelle calls on another child.]

Michelle: Jason, would you like to share?

Jason: Yes, thank you. I never knew that ladybugs squirt a bad-smelling liquid when they get scared. I thought they flew away to get away from danger. Any comments or questions?

Maria: Cool! I didn't know they could do that!

Ansel: That's how they protect themselves!

You did such a thoughtful job of inferring and visualizing from the features and text and learned so much. You combined clues in the text with your background knowledge to make inferences and learn more about the ladybug life cycle. Don't forget to look at our number sentence if it helps you remember how to make an inference! Let's put your Post-its up on the poster so we can see all your great thinking!

Did your students:

■ learn the language of inferring and visualizing and use it to describe their inner conversation?

■ combine their background knowledge with clues from the text to make reasonable inferences?

■ talk about, draw, and record what they inferred and visualized to facilitate learning from informational text?

Reflect& Assess

Young kids convey a great deal of information verbally and through their illustrations. We confer with the kids about their thinking and support them to write down their thoughts. They need lots of oral discussion to practice the strategies of visualizing and inferring. Given that kids' oral comments are more elaborate than what they can write, assessing what they say is important. In some cases, kids' artwork demonstrates learning more clearly than their written responses. In the following work samples, drawing plays an important role in the service of understanding. When assessing emergent readers and writers, we carefully study their drawings and ask them to explain the thinking behind them. This gives us a clear sense of what they think and understand.

Adapt& Differentiate

This lesson was done with first graders, but here are suggestions for how to adapt and differentiate for the whole range of learners.

Younger children who are emergent readers can do the whole lesson by viewing photographs and listening to short sections of the text, such as captions. I would use only part of the *TFK* "Ladybugs" text or an even simpler text, as long as kids could infer from the photographs or pictures. For this lesson, I would probably keep most of the group up close for the guided practice, sending off a few kids who I noticed were ready to try this on their own.

Second graders, such as Joshua and Amanda (see assessment section for their work) are more able to read, view, and infer from texts on their own. They also compose more elaborate inferences and illustrations and fill in the gaps that the text leaves to the reader to figure out. Some children use inferring and visualizing to expand their thinking about the text. This sophisticated thinking seems to occur at the same time as kids notice new information and ask questions. We look for evidence that more developed readers use all the thinking and learning strategies they have been taught to help them acquire knowledge.

1 Michelle's detailed drawings demonstrate her thinking about the growing ladybug. On the first Post-it, she drew a pupa on a leaf and said, "The pupa is on the leaf." On the second Post-it, she drew an adult ladybug and inferred that it is "looking for food because it is hungry" (information that she shared orally). In the final Post-it, Michelle drew her mind picture and commented, "The ladybug eats aphids on a leaf."

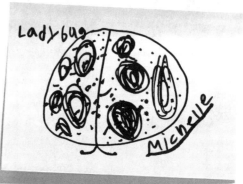

2 Bergen's inference on her first Post-it—that ladybug "eggs are tiny when they are born"—is information inferred from the photographs. Her second Post-it, based on the photos and text, shows she is on the right track that "ladybugs can eat up to 100 aphids." We discuss the idea that it may be difficult to find out exactly how many.

3 An emergent writer, this student illustrated his inference in the first Post-it, saying, "I think birds eat ladybugs," and drew an arrow from the bird to the ladybug. He noted that he learned this from a photograph. When I asked him about his inference, he told me that he knew birds eat lots of kinds of insects and he thought they probably ate ladybugs. We discussed that we could look up this information to confirm it. He also drew what he learned on a second Post-it and said: "I learned ladybugs lay eggs on a leaf."

4 Questioning and inferring are closely related. Kimberly tried to fill a gap in her knowledge by asking, "How did the mom put the eggs on a leaf?" a question I transcribed for her. The article didn't explain this, so she looked for information about insects laying eggs. Kimberly used the strategy of asking questions taught in previous lessons. I am always looking for evidence that kids continue to use strategies they know, developing a repertoire of strategies for understanding nonfiction.

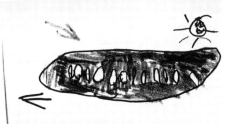

How did the mom put the eggs on the leaf? Kimberly

Independent Practice Post-its

5 Jason found additional information about ladybugs. He was quite excited to report that "when danger is near, a ladybug squirts a bad-smelling liquid" to protect itself and shared his learning with the class. He drew what he visualized, saying that he used to think that ladybugs "just flew away to get away from enemies." We celebrated this new learning and talked about how exciting it is when reading changes thinking!

wen Danger is nere a ladybug Sqerts a bad

Semelling Lecwed.

6 Joshua learned some amazing information from both words and pictures as he read a book on his own. He combined his background knowledge about how animals protect themselves to infer beyond the information given. He combined his background knowledge with text information that when a beetle shoots out chemicals, this causes an attacker to run away. He understood this behavior protects the beetle. We celebrate children who "read between the lines" and gain a further understanding of the information through inferring.

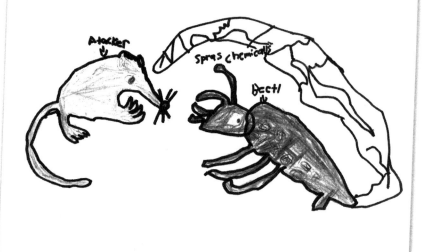

7 (next page, top) Citlalli was reading about desert animals and where they live. Although the illustrations in the book showed the gila monster and the fox alongside their prey—an insect and a jack rabbit, respectively—the words said nothing about this. So she drew inferences from the pictures and wrote up her thinking. Kids are great observers who think and look carefully as they read informational text, and we encourage them to elaborate on what they learn by merging their thinking with the information.

8 (next page, bottom) Amanda, a more developed reader, organized her thinking about her independent reading. Her responses to information about mountain lions included what she learned, "Mountain lions usually hunt at dusk or dawn," as well as questions about when they catch their food and how much they eat. She drew an arrow from her question about when mountain lions catch their food to what she learned, her answer. We are thrilled when kids, like Amanda, begin to use thinking strategies as tools for learning. After reading about mountain lions killing and eating a large deer, she inferred her conclusion, "I think mountain lions eat a lot." We revisited her question about how much they eat "each day" and found out that while mountain lions may eat a lot at once, they may not eat every day. In this way, Amanda came away with more accurate information.

I think that the fox if going to eat a Jack rabet.

Gila monster

I learned that a Gila monster Lives in the Desert. I think a Gila monster eat's Some insects.

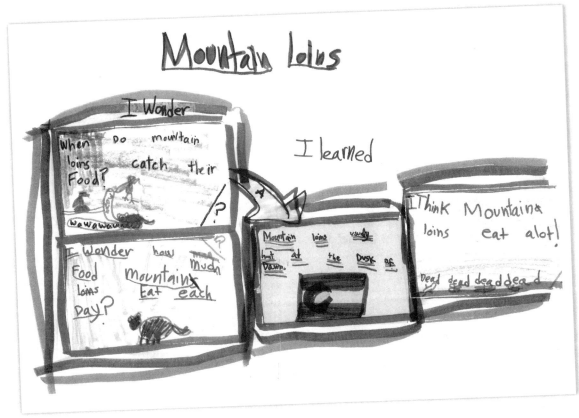

Mountain Loins

I Wonder

When Do mountain loins catch their Food? wawawawa ?

I Wonder how much Food mountains loins Eat each Day?

I learned

Mountain loins usudy hunt at the Dusk of Dawn.

I Think Mountaina loins eat alot! Dead dead dead dead

Make Sense of New Information

Infer from features, pictures, and words

TEACHING MOVES	TEACHING LANGUAGE
	Connect and Engage
Share inferences and elicit kids' thinking about the cover photograph.	■ Let's take a look at this incredible photograph of…. Listen to the title of this text…. When I think about the title and the photo, I infer that the text will be about….
	■ Turn and talk about something you noticed. Start your thought with "I infer" or "I think."
Teach and draw the inference equation.	■ We combine the text clues with our background knowledge to make an inference.
Ask kids to turn and talk about the features they notice.	■ Turn and talk about some of the features you notice on this page. Then we'll share what some of them are. What features did you find?
	Model
Show kids how we infer, combining background knowledge with clues from the words and photos to make meaning.	■ I'm going to read the next page and use phrases like "I think" and "I infer" to combine my BK with clues from the photographs and text. I am using…as clues from the text and I infer….
Have kids turn and talk about photos and features using the phrases "I think," "I infer," and "I visualize."	■ Now you turn and talk about what you see. Be sure to use "I think," "I infer," and "I visualize" in your comments.
Use an example from a child to demonstrate how to make an inference.	■ How interesting! The words didn't tell what was happening, so you had to infer from the picture.
Show how to infer the meaning of an unfamiliar word and mark a Post-it with an *I* for *inference*.	■ I'm not sure what…means, so I'm going to read the words, look at the picture, and see if I can infer the meaning of the word.
	Guide
Invite kids to turn and talk and then share their inferences.	■ Take a look at the picture, think about what you know, and then turn and talk to someone about your thinking. Don't forget to talk about the picture that the words or features create in your mind.
Encourage kids to notice features and text that demonstrate sequence.	■ Who noticed something interesting about one of the features in this text? …please share. This is such an important observation. This feature helps readers to….
Reiterate the language of inferring and visualizing and tie it to the features.	■ Who else wants to share? Thank you. Everyone notice how we are all using language that helps us create pictures in our minds about what we are reading.

The Teaching Moves outline your instructional sequence and the
Teaching Language gives you an idea about what to say to your students.

TEACHING LANGUAGE	TEACHING MOVES
Practice Independently	
▪ Now it's your turn to draw or write your thinking on a Post-it and start your thought with "I think," "I infer," or "I visualize."	Invite kids to write down and/or draw their inferences, saying "I think," "I infer," or "I visualize."
Share the Learning	
▪ Who would like to share? Good for you. Let's notice what…did as a reader and a learner. You said, "I infer…" and "I visualize…" to show how you were using your background knowledge to understand the text.	Encourage kids to share their learning—using the language of visualizing and inferring.
▪ You did a thoughtful job of inferring and visualizing from the pictures, features, and words. Let's put up your Post-its so we can see all your great thinking.	Wrap up the lesson by asking kids to put their Post-its up for all to see.

Reflect & Assess

Did your students:

- ▪ learn the language of inferring and visualizing and use it to describe their inner conversation?

- ▪ combine their background knowledge with clues from the text to make reasonable inferences?

- ▪ talk about, draw, and record what they inferred and visualized to facilitate learning from informational text?

Infer and Visualize with Narrative Nonfict

Text Matters

Narrative nonfiction picture books engage kids because they offer thought-provoking illustrations and information as well as a compelling story. Because we want kids to make thoughtful inferences and to visualize, we look for books with some ambiguity and room for interpretation. Kids can infer the meaning of unfamiliar vocabulary by using the context of the story to support their thinking. We teach them to pay attention to words, pictures, events, and ideas, tying their thinking and mental images to the text and making reasonable inferences rather than wild guesses. Narrative nonfiction books that raise important issues often leave readers with lingering questions at the end—puzzles that push us toward more reading and research.

Resources & Materials

Lesson Text

Antarctica by Helen Cowcher (Farrar, Straus and Giroux, 1990) [Available in the Trade Book Pack.]

Classroom Supplies

- *I Learned/I Inferred* Anchor Chart
- Globe
- Post-its
- Marker

Student Supplies

- Clipboard with Post-its or Post-its Thinksheets [See *Strategy Book 4*, pages 70–71, or the DVD-ROM.]
- Pencil

Tie thinking to the text

Goals& Assessment

We want students to:

- combine their background knowledge with text and picture clues to draw inferences, make predictions, and visualize with narrative nonfiction.

- draw inferences and create mind pictures in response to information, unfamiliar vocabulary, and the story.

- infer big ideas and consider lingering questions prompted by the text.

Why&What

This lesson encourages kids to use inferring and visualizing to make sense of information, the narrative thread of the story, and unfamiliar vocabulary. The lesson is conducted as a read-aloud with guided discussion that elicits inferential thinking as kids listen to the text. As they talk about their inferences, mind pictures, and predictions, we scribe kids' thoughts on the *I Learned/I Inferred* Anchor Chart to record their evolving thinking. As kids anticipate and predict what may happen as the story unfolds, we discuss inferring as "thinking ahead" to try to figure out what's going to happen. Children also infer answers to questions that arise during reading and discuss lingering questions that remain even after finishing the story.

How

Connect and Engage

- Visualize and imagine the story setting to create mind pictures and sensory images before introducing the story.
- Sketch and review the inference equation.
- Introduce *narrative nonfiction*—books that have true information and tell a story.

Model

- Demonstrate how to make an inference based on background knowledge and what was learned from the text and pictures.
- Have kids respond to the text and share inferences as you record them.

Guide

- Guide kids to act out and infer the meaning of unfamiliar vocabulary.
- Guide kids to make inferences about unfamiliar information.
- Use examples from the kids to discuss inferences, visualizations, and predictions about the story and information in the text.

Collaborate

- Encourage children to draw or write what they learned or inferred on Post-its.
- Continue reading, stopping periodically to let kids turn and talk, and then respond.
- Move around the room, conferring with kids as they draw and write responses.

Share the Learning

- Finish reading the story and consider the big ideas.
- Discuss a *lingering question* posed at the end of the story.

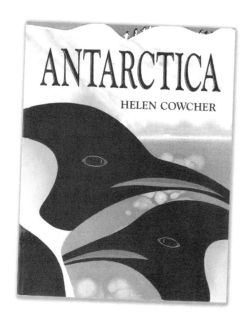

Lesson Text

Antarctica by Helen Cowcher mesmerizes young children with its vivid pictures of this frigid continent and the animals that live there. This nonfiction narrative packs in lots of interesting information about the animals and the difficulty of surviving in one of the world's harshest habitats. The colorful language and illustrations, along with the sophisticated vocabulary, invite kids to combine their background knowledge with text clues to both infer and visualize in response to the text. The book ends with a lingering question, which keeps kids thinking long after they have finished the story.

TEACHING MOVES	TEACHING LANGUAGE

Connect and Engage

Visualize and imagine the story setting to create mind pictures and sensory images before introducing the story.

We're going to take a long trip today! Close your eyes for a minute and imagine a very, very cold place. The wind is whistling and almost knocking you over. The snow is swirling around you, hitting your face, stinging it, and it's difficult to see. You are standing on crunchy snow, and in the distance you can see giant icebergs floating in the ocean. Think about what it would be like to live in such a place!

Now take a look. *[I point to Antarctica on the globe.]* Here is where we are—the continent of Antarctica—down at the bottom of the earth, at the South Pole. Turn and talk: What were you visualizing, feeling, and imagining just now, standing there on the ice and snow? What do you already know about Antarctica? Turn and talk. *[Kids chat for a few minutes and then share out.]*

TIP: This lessson is done with narrative nonfiction—true information written in story form. This genre encourages readers to use inferring and visualizing, strategies often used to understand stories and narratives.

Alicia: It's freezing! You'd have to wear one hundred coats!

Benji: It's a whiteout! That's a big blizzard.

Jillian: There are no trees, no rocks, no people. Nothing. Just snow and ice.

Joshua: Actually, penguins live there. I saw that penguin movie. There are a *lot* of penguins. And seals, too. The penguins just stand on the ice, no matter how cold it gets.

Dane: If it is so windy, how can the animals live on the ice?

Your descriptions are making me shiver! You have vivid mind pictures, and you know so many interesting things about Antarctica. And you are curious; you asked an interesting question. We're going to use all your great background knowledge today to figure out what's going on in this book. *[I hold up Antarctica.]* Do you remember the picture I drew that shows what we do when we make an inference?

TEACHING LANGUAGE   **TEACHING MOVES**

I'm going to sketch a person making an inference. *[I sketch and review the inference equation—from Lesson 14.]* Remember, we said we combine our background knowledge with what we learn from the pictures and words in the text. That's how we make an inference. You have gotten really good at making inferences and creating mind pictures, and we're going to do more of that today, OK?

For the next day or two we're going to be reading this book: *Antarctica.* As you listen, think about the pictures, the information, and what's happening in the story. That's a lot to do at once, but I know you can do it! This book is interesting because it is a story and it also has a lot of information about the animals that live in Antarctica and how they survive in such an incredibly cold climate. When a book has both information and a story, we call it *narrative nonfiction.* In this story, the author doesn't always tell us exactly what's happening.

Joshua: So we have to figure it out.

Exactly, Joshua. That's what we're going to do. I've noticed that when I have to figure out what's going on in a story, by visualizing and inferring, the book really grabs and keeps my attention. I just want to keep on reading and not stop. I know you all will be very interested in this story, so let's get going.

Sketch and review the inference equation.

pictures and words / text clues + background knowledge / what we know = an inference

Introduce narrative nonfiction—*books that have true information and tell a story.*

Model

Let's look at the cover. *[I hold up the book.]* Look at these striking illustrations of these emperor penguins! Be thinking about what you already know about Antarctica and the animals, like penguins, that live there. *[I turn to the first page and begin reading.]*

In the cold far south, in Antarctica, live emperor penguins, Weddell seals, and Adelie penguins.

So these are some of the animals that live there. I'll keep reading.

The emperor penguin lays her egg in winter, when it is dark both day and night. Then she leaves to feed at sea.

Jamie: Look at the picture. I think that's the dad with the egg on his feet!

Hold your thought for a moment, Jamie, and we'll stop to talk after I read the next sentence.

While she is gone, her mate carefully nestles the egg on top of his feet for two months.

Jamie: Told you so!

Jamie, you made a great inference using the text, the picture, and your background knowledge. You inferred that the male penguin was holding the egg on his feet—and the text confirmed your inference. That means you were right on! Such amazing information; two months is a long time to stand there

Demonstrate how to make an inference based on background knowledge and what was learned from the text and pictures.

with an egg on your feet! *[I point to the* I Learned/I Inferred *Anchor Chart.]* Do you see this column on the Anchor Chart? It says *I Learned.* I'm going to draw a picture of the male penguin holding the egg on his feet—and write what we learned. *[I sketch a penguin with an egg.]*

I'm thinking about the information I just wrote—that the male penguin holds the egg on his feet. I've got some background knowledge about penguins and their eggs. I know that eggs have to be kept warm if the animal inside it is going to hatch. I'm going to combine what I know about eggs staying warm with what I learned about the penguin holding the egg on his feet to make an inference: *I infer* the penguin must be keeping the egg warm so it will hatch. And I'll write that down in the *I Inferred* column because it's my inference.

Have kids respond to the text and share inferences as you record them.

Turn and talk about your thoughts. Start your comment with words that show you are inferring. Say "I think," or "I infer," or "I visualize." Then we'll share. *[After a minute or two, kids share out and I record their thinking on the* I Learned/I Inferred *Anchor Chart.]*

Dane: I think he puts the egg under a flap near his feet.

Lani: I infer that the egg won't break; it stays safe.

Benji: If the dad didn't hold it, maybe it would roll away and fall in the water.

Such great inferences! You had inferences about what we learned—the fact that the male penguin holds the egg on his feet—because you have some background knowledge about this. You combined your background knowledge with the words and picture in the text to make an inference. And you all used language that signals inferential thinking: "I think," "I infer," and "Maybe." Now we understand more about how the egg is kept warm and safe until it hatches.

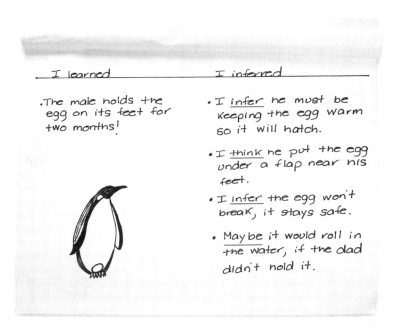

Guide

OK, let's stand up! We're going to act out what the penguins are doing in the story. Let's do what we see the penguins doing in this picture. That's right. We're going to stand really close together as we read this part. *[I read the part where the penguins huddle as we act out the word* huddle.*]*

Now you see how we can use a picture to infer the meaning of a word. We all know what the word "huddle" means because we acted it out! The penguins bunch up together to stay warm! *[I add "male penguins huddle" and write the meaning of the word in the* I Inferred *column.]*

I'll read more now. Think about what we learn and what we infer from the story. Remember the male is still holding the egg on his feet as he huddles in a tight circle to stay warm. *[I continue reading.]*

> *Meanwhile, his mate is feeding at sea...where danger lurks.*

I'm inferring from the picture and words that the female penguin has gone to find food in the ocean. *[I record this on the chart.]*

Gina: What does that mean—"where danger lurks"?

That's a good question, Gina. Let's figure out what these words mean. I think that the words "where danger lurks" are telling us that it's dangerous for the female penguin in the ocean. *Lurking* means the same as *hiding and waiting*

Guide kids to act out and infer the meaning of unfamiliar vocabulary.

I learned	I inferred
• The male holds the egg on its feet for two months!	• I infer he must be keeping the egg warm so it will hatch.
	• I think he put the egg under a flap near his feet.
	• I infer the egg won't break, it stays safe.
	• Maybe it would roll in the water, if the dad didn't hold it.
• Male penguins huddle.	• "Huddle" means to bunch up together in a tight circle.
• Female (mom) feeding at sea.	• I infer she's gone to find food in the ocean.
• "where danger lurks" – it's dangerous for the female in the ocean.	• I think an animal that hunts penguins is waiting to eat the female.

for. So I infer an animal that hunts penguins is swimming in the water and waiting to catch and eat it.

Turn and talk about an inference you are making, from either the words or the picture. *[Kids turn and talk and then share with the large group.]*

Jamie: I am thinking that the danger could be a killer whale.

Alicia: I think it's a shark.

Ellen: But sharks don't live there; it's too cold.

These are really reasonable inferences. Let's keep reading and see if your inferences are confirmed. *[I turn the page—to reveal a giant picture of a leopard seal in the water.]* Oh, my goodness, look at this picture. It says: *A ferocious leopard seal!* That's a fierce, dangerous seal. That's what *ferocious* means. The animal waiting for the penguin was a leopard seal, not a killer whale or a shark.

Jamie: But I know killer whales eat penguins.

Exactly, Jamie. You've got some accurate background knowledge. It could have been a killer whale waiting in the water to eat that penguin. In this case, though, it was a leopard seal waiting to catch that unsuspecting penguin!

Frankie: But what's going to happen?

Interesting question. I think we are all wondering that. That's why this is a good story; we are curious about what's going to happen, and we keep thinking ahead about what might come next. That's called making a *prediction*. We infer and think ahead about what's going to happen in the story. Turn and talk about your predictions. What do you predict is going to happen next in the story?

Benji: That leopard seal wants to eat the penguin; it's chasing her!

Lani: I bet he doesn't catch it!

Gina: I think he does. Leopard seals are fast, and maybe the penguin didn't see him coming.

Dane: We don't know if the leopard seal caught it or not.

All of your predictions about what's going to happen between the leopard seal and the penguin are reasonable—that's because you're combining what you already know about hunting and animals with the text clues. You are really tying your predictions and inferences to the information in the text to make sense of it. Let's read to find out what does happen:

> **Luck is with the emperor penguin this time. She leaves the water safely and trudges back to the rookery.**

Jordan: The penguin was lucky because she escaped from the seal. I think she jumped up on the ice just in time.

Let's go back and reread the part that Jordan is talking about. *[I reread the page.]* Tell us about your thinking here, Jordan.

Jordan: The penguin mom got up onto the ice. She was lucky that the leopard seal didn't catch her. Here she is in the picture. *[Jordan points to the penguin on the ice.]*

Exactly. Jordan inferred from the text and picture that the female penguin was very lucky to escape from the leopard seal. From the picture we see that she escaped onto the ice, just as you said, Jordan. So some of you found that your predictions were confirmed. But some of us thought the leopard seal would catch and eat the penguin because we know leopard seals do that. That's a good possibility, but it didn't happen here. All of your predictions were thoughtful ones—it's just how the story turns out. Sometimes our predictions come true, sometimes they don't.

Benji: I visualized a picture of a penguin swimming and jumping up onto the ice.

Let's listen as Benji describes what the penguin did to get up onto the ice. Let's create our own mind pictures.

Benji: It was swimming in the water and all of a sudden it jumped onto the ice—but it landed on its belly and slid! *[I ask Benji to act this out to show us.]*

Thanks, Benji, for helping us visualize how the penguin escaped onto the ice. Benji helped me create a mind picture of those swimming, jumping, sliding penguins! You all have done a great job of inferring, predicting, and visualizing because you have tied your thinking to the text and pictures.

> **Use examples from the kids to discuss inferences, visualizations, and predictions about the story and information in the text.**

Collaborate

[I hand out Post-its, pencils, and clipboards so that kids can respond as I keep reading Antarctica.] Take a minute to talk with someone near you and then write or draw something you inferred or visualized from the story. You can start your Post-it with the words *I learned* or *I inferred*. If you need some help spelling these words, they are right here. *[I point to I Learned/I Inferred Anchor Chart.]*

[To be responsive to these kindergarteners' needs and engagement level, I break up the interactive read-aloud, continuing to read the story the next day.]

Now let's continue reading our book, *Antarctica*. Who remembers what happened last?

Ella: The mother penguin escaped from the bad seal.

That's right, Ella. Now we'll read on to see what happens next. When I read, I'll stop from time to time to let you write or draw your thinking.

[We stop every few pages for them to talk with a partner and record their thinking in words or pictures, and I circulate, conferring with kids.]

> **Encourage children to draw or write what they learned or inferred on Post-its.**
>
> **TIP:** Reading the story over two or even three sessions keeps the kids engaged and focused. Older, more developed readers may be able to listen to and respond to the story in one sitting.
>
> **Continue reading, stopping periodically to let kids turn and talk and then respond.**
>
> **Move around the room, conferring with kids as they draw and write responses.**

Share the Learning

Finish reading the story and consider the big ideas.

Let's read the last page.

The penguins and the seals have always shared their world with ancient enemies, the skuas and the leopard seals. But these new arrivals are more dangerous. The seals and penguins cannot tell yet whether they will share or destroy their beautiful Antarctica...

Whoa—there is a lot going on here. Let's think through these words and see if we can figure out what is happening. I think there is an important idea the author is trying to tell us. I'm thinking the first sentence is telling important information when it says that the penguins and seals have always shared their world with ancient enemies. It tells us that the animals of Antarctica have always had natural enemies. Animals have always survived by eating other animals. We were shocked to see that the skua birds live by eating penguin eggs, but the eggs are the birds' food. We were relieved to see the penguin get away from the leopard seal, but we know that leopard seals depend on penguins as a source of food, just like penguins depend on fish for their food. That's a big idea—that animals survive in habitats where they can find food. Natural enemies—the animals that eat them—are a part of that habitat.

But what about this next part? Turn and talk about what you infer is happening here. Then we'll share your thoughts out with the whole group. *[I reread, beginning with* But these new arrivals are more dangerous....*]*

Ian: I think there's a clue in the picture. There is a boat, so maybe it's the boats with people.

Ella: The people in the helicopters, they are new. They scared all those penguins away, so the babies got eaten by those birds!

Lizette: I infer the animals don't know what is going on.

Jared: I saw on TV that people study Antarctica. They study the animals and the ice and everything.

These are some really interesting thoughts. You combined your background knowledge with clues in the text to infer that the humans are the new arrivals and may cause problems for the animals. I've got some information related to your background knowledge, Jared. You know that scientists study and do research in Antarctica. And I know that Antarctica is a protected continent. That means that there are laws to prevent people from harming the environment or the animals while they are visiting or doing research there.

Discuss a *lingering question* posed at the end of the story.

I'm going to reread the last sentence once more because it's really important. *[I reread.]* The seals and penguins cannot tell yet whether they will share or destroy their beautiful Antarctica. This sentence makes me think of a question. My question is, "Will the people coming to Antarctica share the environment with the animals, or will they change the environment in ways that destroy it?" This is what we call a *lingering question*, because it is a question I want to learn more about and investigate further.

You did a great job thinking through this book. If you have some last thoughts, inferences, or questions, write them on Post-its and we'll share them out with the whole group.

Based on what we just read, I'm wondering what is being done to protect Antarctica and its animals. If you are interested in researching this question, we could find out more information in the library and on the Internet. We'll get a small group together, do some research, and come back to the rest of the class with what we find out. That's why we do research, to teach and share our new learning with everyone.

TIP: When we see that some of our kids are especially captivated by a topic, we support them in forming small-group inquiries, where they can pursue answers to their burning questions right away. And we provide them with a curious audience to come back to when they've gathered new information and answers.

Reflect& Assess

This lesson was done in a kindergarten classroom, so we scribed the kids' thinking during the lesson and conferences, writing down their oral language to capture the full scope of their thinking. We often scribe kids' thinking because their reasoning is far more sophisticated than they are able to write themselves. But we're careful to encourage kids to draw and write down as much as they can independently, letting them take over as soon as they are ready.

When kids have considerable background knowledge on a topic, as these kids had about penguins and other animals from Antarctica, they make many inferences and the discussion moves in the direction of big ideas and issues. When children do not have specific background knowledge about a topic, they often base their inferences on life experiences and more general knowledge. In either case, we find kids are eager to use their general knowledge about, and experience in, the world to infer. We support children to refine their inferences rather than make wild guesses, guiding them to make sure they tie their thinking to the text.

Adapt& Differentiate

This lesson was done with kindergarteners, but here are suggestions for how to adapt and differentiate for the whole range of learners.

With kindergarteners, the entire lesson is an interactive read-aloud. We guide kids to draw and write responses as we read the book out loud. We stop frequently to encourage kids to turn, talk, and write or draw their thinking. In this way, the lesson often takes several sessions. I guide the kids through the final pages of the story and share my thinking about the big ideas and lingering questions that the ambiguous ending prompts.

With older, more experienced readers, I give them a chance to weigh in with their thoughts at the end of the story—letting them figure out and reason through the culminating events and draw their own inferences and interpretations. Work samples are included from second graders who had a lot of background knowledge about some of the animals in the story and who sought out more information about the laws protecting Antarctica's habitat.

Kindergarten Responses

1 Tyrone wrote, "I think penguins fear leopard seals." Tyrone's inference made sense, given the suspenseful point in the story where the penguin barely escapes being eaten by the leopard seal. Narrative nonfiction often invites kids to view animals in more human terms, so it is important to clarify the difference between animal behavior and human emotions. I return to this topic with Tyrone in a conference, and we discuss the fact that animals act on what we call instincts, while people have feelings and emotions, such as fear.

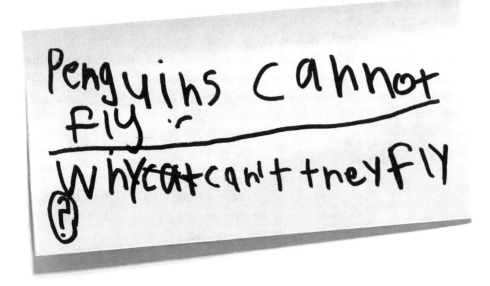

2 As kids learn new information, they often wonder about it. This child's question about why penguins can't fly followed his new learning. He answered his own question as he wrote down his inference that penguins don't have wings after all. They have flippers. We are thrilled to see kids keep track of their unfolding thinking—and how it changes in the face of new information.

I think... they cuddle up together to stay warm.

BY LANI

I wonder... why they all cuddle up together?

3 Lani wondered why penguins "all cuddle up together?," a question I scripted for her. She responded, "I think they cuddle up together to stay warm." As I wrote Lani's question and thinking, I reviewed the word *huddle* from the lesson, and we discussed the difference between cuddling and huddling. When we confer with kids, we encourage their attempts to think through the text but at the same time model more precise language to make sure that kids gain accurate information.

These children inferred information about the animals, combining their background knowledge with what they learned from the book. As more experienced readers and writers, they record and illustrate more extensive thinking prompted by the story and the information in it. The picture caption, "In this picture the dad is giving the baby penguin onto the mom's feet very, very gently," uses a text feature to clarify thinking.

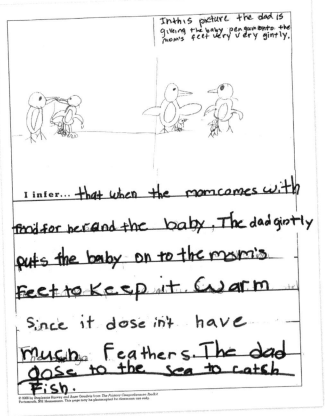

I thinkTHaT The People chud NotleveTHeir Trash in ANTARCTICA Because THaT might Be dangerous Foa Pehguins.

Name Alejandra Date 11/28/07

I learned that you can not be next to a peng uin Yecause you will distrb it. You can stay back 100feet

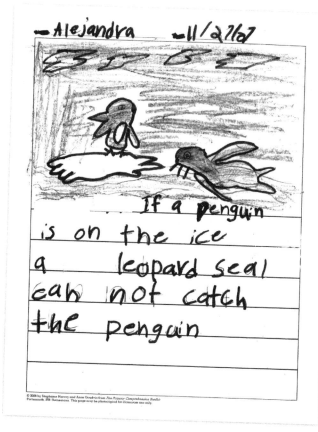

-Alejandra -11/27/07

If a penguin is on the ice a leopard seal can not catch the penguin

These children all learned new information from reading *Antarctica* and went on to do more research on both the animals and the ecological issues that arise when people come to a fragile habitat. Then they wrote about and illustrated their new learning.

Infer and Visualize with Narrative Nonfiction

Tie thinking to the text

TEACHING MOVES	TEACHING LANGUAGE
	Connect and Engage
Visualize and imagine the story setting to create mind pictures and sensory images before introducing the story.	▪ We're going to read a great book today, but first close your eyes and imagine…. Think about what it would be like to…. Turn and talk about what you were thinking and imagining.
	▪ What pictures did you see in your mind? Your descriptions make me feel….
	▪ We're going to use all your background knowledge today to figure out what's going on in this text.
Sketch and review the inference equation.	▪ Remember we said we combine what we learn from pictures and words with our background knowledge to make an inference? Here is the inference equation that I have drawn for you.
Introduce *narrative nonfiction*— books that have true information and tell a story.	▪ We are going to be reading about…. As you listen, think about the pictures, the information, and what's happening in the story. When a book has both information and a story, we call it narrative nonfiction.
	▪ In this story, the author doesn't always tell us exactly what is happening. So we have to figure it out by inferring and visualizing.
	Model
Demonstrate how to make an inference based on background knowledge and what was learned from the text and pictures.	▪ Let's look at the cover, and then I'll begin reading. I'll stop so we can talk after a few sentences.
	▪ What can you infer from this picture? That's a great inference… and we read some words that confirmed what you thought.
	▪ Let's write that inference down in the *I Inferred* column….
Have kids respond to the text and share inferences as you record them.	▪ Now I'm going to read some more…. Turn and talk about your thoughts. Start your comment with words like "I think," "I infer," or "I visualize." Then we'll share.
	▪ Such great inferences! You had inferences about what we learned because you had some background knowledge about this.
	▪ I'll jot down your inferences on the *I Learned/I Inferred* Anchor Chart.

LESSON GUIDE

The Teaching Moves outline your instructional sequence and the
Teaching Language gives you an idea about what to say to your students.

TEACHING LANGUAGE	TEACHING MOVES

Guide

- What do you infer the word…means from this picture? Let's act out what the word means.

  Guide kids to act out and infer the meaning of unfamiliar vocabulary.

- I'll read more now…. Turn and talk about an inference you are making, from either the words or the pictures.

  Guide kids to make inferences about unfamiliar information.

- These are really thoughtful inferences. Let's keep reading and see if your inferences are confirmed.

- See, some of your inferences came true and others didn't. When we make a prediction, we infer and think ahead about what's going to happen in the story. Then we can confirm if this happens or not.

  Use examples from the kids to discuss inferences, visualizations, and predictions about the story and information in the text.

- All of your predictions and inferences are reasonable because you have tied your thinking to the text. But a story can always go in different ways from what we infer and predict.

Collaborate

- Take a minute to draw or write what we have been talking about or something you inferred or visualized from the story.

  Encourage children to draw or write what they learned or inferred on Post-its.

- I will continue reading, and you draw or write what comes to mind, OK? I will stop now and then to talk with you.

  Continue reading, stopping periodically to let kids turn and talk and then respond.

- I will walk around and confer with you. Does anyone need help?

  Move around the room, conferring with kids as they draw and write responses.

Share the Learning

- Let's read the last page. Let's think through these words and see if we can figure out what is happening.

  Finish reading the story and consider the big ideas.

- The last part…makes me think of a question. The question is…. This is what we call a *lingering question*—one we can think about and investigate further.

  Discuss a lingering question posed at the end of the story.

Reflect & Assess

Did your students:

- combine their background knowledge with text and picture clues to draw inferences, make predictions, and visualize with narrative nonfiction?

- draw inferences and create mind pictures in response to information, unfamiliar vocabulary, and the story?

- infer big ideas and consider lingering questions prompted by the text?

Infer and Visualize Strategy Wrap-up:
Creating an Anchor Chart to Capture What We Learned about Inferring and Visualizing

Teaching Language

Now that we have done some lessons on inferring and visualizing when we read and view, let's take a look back at what we have learned. We can co-construct an Anchor Chart about this strategy that will serve as a visual reminder and help us to infer and visualize. The *Inferring and Visualizing* Anchor Chart can help guide us as we continue thinking about how to use inferring and visualizing to help us understand what we read.

I'll begin by sharing something important that I do when I infer and visualize, and I will record it on the chart. When I read, listen, or view, I think about what I know and merge it with text clues to make meaning. I also get a picture in my mind of what I am reading. While I am jotting this down on the chart, turn to each other and talk about something you have learned about inferring and visualizing that is important to think about when we read. Be sure to say it in a way that makes sense to you.

[Kids turn and talk.]

Let's share some of your thoughts. *[We want to capture kids' comments that show their understanding of the strategy as well as our lesson language to guide future teaching and learning.]*

What We Learned about Inferring and Visualizing

We think about what we know and merge our background knowledge with text clues to make meaning.

We visualize by getting a picture in our mind of the story or poem.

We make inferences from the pictures to get information.

We infer from the features to get information.

We visualize from the features to get information.

We infer the meaning of unfamiliar words and concepts.

We infer ahead in the story and make predictions.

We tie inferences and mental images to the information and pictures in the text.

We infer and visualize from the text and pictures in a story to better understand it.

Assessment Checklist for Infer and Visualize

Expectations for student thinking and learning

- Merge background knowledge with text clues to make meaning
- Get a picture in their mind as they listen, read, and view
- Understand what it means to infer
- Understand what it means to visualize
- Infer from the features to get information
- Infer to make and confirm predictions
- Figure out the meaning of unfamiliar words by using the context
- Infer from text and pictures to understand the story

Questions you can ask yourself to assess student understanding

- Are they using their background knowledge and merging it with text clues to make meaning?
- Do they get pictures in their minds as they read, listen, and view?
- Do they understand what it means to infer?
- Do they understand what it means to visualize?
- Do they get information by inferring from the text features?
- Do they infer the meaning of unfamiliar words and concepts by using the context?
- Do they infer and visualize from the text and pictures to more fully understand the story?

Language of inferring and visualizing

"I infer…"

"I'm inferring…"

"I visualize…"

"I'm visualizing…"

"I think…"

"I'm thinking…"

"Maybe…"

"Maybe it means…"

"It seems to me…"

"Probably…"

"I am getting a picture…"

"I can see…"

"I have a picture in my head…"

Annotated Rubric for Strategy Book 4:
Infer and Visualize

Name _____

Date _____

Oral and/or Written Evidence	Strong Evidence 3	Some Evidence 2	Little Evidence 1
Merges background knowledge with text clues to make meaning			
Creates mental images (visualizes) while reading, listening, and viewing			
Infers and visualizes from features and pictures			
Infers the meaning of unfamiliar words and concepts			
Infers from text and pictures to understand the story			

Name _____ Date _____

I infer...

Name _____   Date _____

I infer...

Name _____   Date _____

I infer...

Name _____ Date _____

Name _____   Date _____